KINDER PEARLS

A Handbook of Education & Character Building of Children for Parents

Written by
Sujata Goel

Illustrated by
Alysaa Kusuma Seth

BLUEROSE PUBLISHERS
India | U.K.

Copyright © Sujata Goel 2025

All rights reserved by author. No part of this publication may be reproduced, stored in a retrieval system or transmitted in any form or by any means, electronic, mechanical, photocopying, recording or otherwise, without the prior permission of the author. Although every precaution has been taken to verify the accuracy of the information contained herein, the publisher assumes no responsibility for any errors or omissions. No liability is assumed for damages that may result from the use of information contained within.

BlueRose Publishers takes no responsibility for any damages, losses, or liabilities that may arise from the use or misuse of the information, products, or services provided in this publication.

For permissions requests or inquiries regarding this publication, please contact:

BLUEROSE PUBLISHERS
www.BlueRoseONE.com
info@bluerosepublishers.com
+91 8882 898 898
+4407342408967

ISBN: 978-93-6452-510-7

Cover Design: Sadhna Kumari
Illustrated By Alysaa Kusuma Seth
Typesetting: Pooja Sharma

First Edition: February 2025

This book is dedicated to

my Mother

Mrs. Swaraj Goel

She was an epitome of inspiration

&

My Grand daughter

Alysaa Kusuma Seth

With Gratitude and Affection.

Testimonial

For years I have been working in this field with adults and children alike.

And while going through the text I found myself wondering, both as a professional and a parent that, somehow most of the practical applications of my work, I found elaborated in each topic the book attempted to address.

Essentially, I found myself thoroughly enjoying the book with all the little "pearls of wisdom" hidden in the anecdotal approach of the author's experience.

In my purview the book provides a vantage point for the parents and professionals in the field of childcare, education, pedagogy, parenting and child psychology.

All in all, it's a must read!

Dr (Lt Col) Neelam Rathi

MBBS, MD (Psychiatry)

Child Psychology (Pursuing), Norway

About the author

Ms. Sujatha is a transformational early year's educator, blogger, a mother and a grandmother.

She has dedicated more than 22 years of her life in the field of education in India and abroad. She started off as a Preschool teacher, then Kindergarten and went on to become Kindergarten head. She held onto one school for 19+ years only because she loves what she does and committed herself totally to it. She is passionate about her work and has contributed in every possible way to the field of early years education.

She joined as a kindergarten teacher in GEMS Modern Academy, Dubai, U.A.E (A premier institution) to enhance her skills and to incorporate knowledge and experience in to a new approach towards learning. She believes that it's never too late to reinvent yourself as an individual. Learning is a lifelong process thus, she wanted to give a different perspective to her pedagogical methodology and grow as a professional as well. She writes blogs, creates new activities and now writing a hand book for kinder parents. She has recently started a Non-Profit Organization named 'ज्ञानShala an Initiative' for the upliftment of the neighbourhood children to make difference.

Prologue

Dear Parents,

Kindergarten is a major turning point in the lives of both, the children and the parents. It is very important to remember that the early school experience has lasting effects on children regarding their attitude about their school, their self-esteem and their achievements.

Getting ready for kindergarten is a fun and exciting time both for the families and children. Children and parents come to kindergarten with a variety of experience and skill levels. This complete guide is planned to give you an idea of what to expect and how you can help your child to get ready.

Fortunately, the best person to ensure that your children arrive at school ready to succeed is you! Becoming involved in your child's educational and developmental process early in life will help them in making a smooth transition into kindergarten.

Hence, here I am presenting a complete guide for you to take a Sneak-Peak in the early years of your child and have also tried to answer 'Why? How? What? And When?'

Contents

1. My journey as a mother and Grandmother 1
2. Parents are partners in their kids learning 2
3. How to make the parenting effective & getting ready for kindergarten 5
4. The smooth transition 9
5. Separation nervousness 12
6. Kindergarten- the wider aspect 16
7. Learning time management... 20
8. Reading Readiness 26
9. Math Readiness.. 30
10. Science readiness 33
11. Role of Art, Music and Physical Education................... 37
12. Important building blocks... 41
13. Conversations that make difference 56
14. It's a big world 71
Epilogue 86

1.
My journey as a mother and Grandmother

"Share your knowledge. It's a way to achieve immortality."

Dalai Lama

As rightly said by Dalai Lama, I would like to share all my experiences as a mother and grandmother.

I brought up my three beautiful children and together we grew up. It's a beautiful divine feeling – so pure and satisfying! The process of learning and teaching go hand in hand, complementing each other.

Being a grandmother is the biggest joy of life!

How to begin and explain the magic that took over when I found out I was going to be a grandparent? Being a grandparent is a treat not everyone is fortunate enough to enjoy. And I also know that watching your grandchildren grow, helps you stay young and active. I am so grateful for the fountain of youth in my life that now comes in the form of two adorable little kids, Alysaa and Axel.

2.
Parents are partners in their kids learning

We should always remember parents and teachers need to work as a team to bring out the best in a child. Parents impact their children's behavior about how they learn at home. Parental involvement has a great effect on the child's success. They are an important connection between home and school. And when they get involved in the school, the schools become better places to learn, grow and bloom. You as parents are your child's most important guardian, and your child's teacher is your partner in educating your child. As it is rightly said by 'Jane D. Hull'.

"At the end of the day, the most overwhelming key to success is the positive involvement of parents."

Visit the classroom more often, talk to the teacher, volunteer at school and, be an active member of the parent involvement programs.

The advantages of parents getting involved in the learning process.

Most importantly, the learning and growing process becomes interesting.

- The learning becomes smooth and simple if the children get encouragement at home.

- They feel stimulated and happy when they see their parents equally involved; hence, they do better and achieve good results.

- Involvement of parents gives them more activities and more help apart from the school.

- Their concerns can be sorted out easily when their parents have a positive relationship with school staff.

- They are pleased when their parents are enjoying events in the school.

- Where there is a positive relationship between parents and their child's school, there are benefits all around.

- Parents get reassurance that their children are receiving a good education and are well informed.

- Another important aspect is that parents can build up their own confidence and skills.

Building positive hopes

Building positive relationships between teachers and parents is very important. Take every opportunity to get to know your child's school and staff. Take your child to play at the playground, attend school events and talk about school as it's the beginning of an exciting new time in their life.

Staying in touch

Communication between parents and school and your child's teacher is the key to success in school. If you have any questions about what your child is doing in school or how your child is doing, schedule a time to talk with the teacher. It will give a sense of satisfaction and confidence.

3.
How to make the parenting effective & getting ready for kindergarten

~ Dalai Lama said, "Give the ones you love wings to fly, roots to come back and reasons to stay." It is such a beautiful thought!

Parents are lucky to have the opportunity to nurture their kids with positivity and love to become better human beings of tomorrow.

Making small changes and teaching our new generation discipline will help develop their routine for going to bed and getting ready for school, doing homework and keeping school papers in a proper place. Help your children become independent in dressing, eating, and personal hygiene. Their routines developed early will pay off for years to come.

Here are some suggestions:

- Establish a bedtime of eight or more hours of sleep each night. Be sure your child is getting enough rest and access to healthy, nutritious food. Healthy kids learn better!

- Children develop at different rates and times. Try not to compare the two siblings or other children.

- If your first language is not English, continue to speak and read to them in your home language. This is important in developing basic academic concepts. Interact frequently with your children by **talking, listening, questioning** and **reasoning.**

- Make sure your child gets plenty of play time outside and away from electronics. Provide opportunities for rigorous physical activity every day and play with other children. Arrange toys, games and household objects that encourage dramatic play, manipulation and investigation.

- **Teach your child how to stay healthy by coughing into his or her elbow, keeping hands away from noses, not sharing drinks, and washing hands a lot.**

- Walking your child into the classroom is fine, but its best to keep goodbyes quick and cheerful. If your child has issues with separation anxiety, let the teacher handle it. Children usually get swept away by the activity in the room.

- Get used to checking your child's backpack often for copies of work or important notices from the teacher.

- Read to your children every day. Talk about the story and pictures. Reading with children does not have to be limited to picture books at their level. Try reading chapter books at a higher level. Use voices. Have fun with it!

- Check the school's lost and found periodically to see if your child has left something behind. Teach your children socially acceptable ways to disagree.

- Talk with your children about your family, your culture and your values. Provide opportunities for your children to learn about other cultures in your community. Encourage social values such as happiness, cooperation, sharing, and concern for others.

- Demonstrate common expressions of courtesy and praise your children for using them. Establish reasonable limits for behavior and hold your children to them.

- Make sure your children have all required immunizations and a current health checkup.

- Take your children to a variety of places such as the library, park, post office, museums, and grocery stores.

- Work often with your children on different skills to encourage small muscle development, eye-hand coordination and creative expression.

- Encourage work values such as effort, persistence and initiative.

- Expose your children to good literature. Provide books, magazines and other printed materials for your children to handle.

- Provide opportunities to play games that recognize and identify numbers.

- Provide your children with pens, pencils, markers and paper. Encourage writing and scribbling.

- Be consistent!

4.

The smooth transition

The word 'transition' means the changeover from nursery to kindergarten. It is understood to be a main milestone not only for the child but for his family as well. The attitude towards school and learning that the child carried with him for life is often determined by this very first experience with school.

To be successful in school, it should be made sure that the child has a smooth transition to kindergarten from nursery. It is important then that parents, childcare providers, and kindergarten teachers work jointly together to minimize the adverse aspects of the transition to kindergarten. If this approach is followed, then it provides lasting benefits for all the people involved.

The benefits of smooth transition for children are:

- Enhanced self-confidence.
- Better relationships with the other children and adults.
- Strong trust between teachers and children.
- Elevated motivation and ready for new experiences.
- Issncreased continuity with earlier educational experiences.

The benefits of smooth transition for parents are:

- There is a vast improvement in their children's confidence to achieve more and learn new things.

- There is an increase in their ongoing development in the educational process.
- Increased self-confidence in their own ability to communicate with teachers and to effectively influence the educational system.

5.
Separation nervousness

Now, this again is a very important part, and it needs a very gentle approach and understanding.

I remember when Alysaa was a little girl, I used to drop her off her school sometimes. She used to cry and was not happy. Though I used to talk to her about it on the way to school and tell her about the activities she would be doing, playing with her friends, and learning new things, but she was still unhappy.

Every child has to learn to cope with temporary separations from their parents. Learning to be apart can be difficult for both parents and children. Though both benefit from spending time with other people.

Many of the children attending school will be unhappy and sad when their parents leave. This is called "separation nervousness" and is often exhibited by usually four- five-years old. In some cases, the discomfort will re-emerge when the parents come to collect the child at the end of the school. This is because the sight of the parent has brought back the memory of being left back in the morning. It can be a very distressing time for parents, children, and teachers as well. Separation nervousness occurs because the child does not feel safe to be away from people they know and trust. Therefore, it is very important to build that trust with the child.

Trust can be built by showing the child that you, the parent, trust the **teacher** and are comfortable leaving your child at school. Spend some time chatting with the teacher while the child plays nearby. When the child sees you trust the teacher, they will begin to trust the teacher too.

The best possible way to handle separation nervousness is to stay positive and encouraging. Do remember to alert the teacher that your child might need some emotional support.

Comfort your child, hug them, kiss them, smile and say 'goodbye, have a happy day' and leave quickly without looking back. Later, you can call and check if he is fine. If the school does not call that means your child has settled well. When you pick up your child from school, please make sure you are on **time** and ask about what they did and help them to look forward to the next kindergarten session.

You must share all the information with the teacher about the child's routine and fears, and the sort of night they had before. This means the school will be well aware of the information about the child. It will help the teachers to build trust in the child and make him feel comfortable.

Remember, separation nervousness is part of many four-five-year old's development. It will in the due run pass if managed well.

How parents can help children at home

There are things parents can do to help children at home and learn to manage their anxious feelings. Parent's support plays an important role in helping kids learn to cope independently. Try these strategies at home to help your child succeed outside of home.

❖ Parents can arrive early to school with kids and can volunteer to help the teacher before the other kids arrive.

- ❖ You can help your child with a list of positive thoughts and let him write these on cards and put in the backpack.
- ❖ Can write daily lunch box notes that include positive phrases.
- ❖ Should avoid overscheduling of planned activities.
- ❖ Focus on playtime, outdoor time, and healthy sleep habits.
- ❖ Alert your child of the change in routine ahead of time.
- ❖ Empathize with your child and don't forget to appreciate the progress they made.

6.

Kindergarten- the wider aspect

You as parents, should always remember that you are your child's **first teacher** and no one else can handle them better than you. Academics are very important in the journey of growth and development of a child. Here are some pointers you can be working on to help get your child ready for the academics.

6. i) Getting the child ready for the Academic Skills

1. Every day, read to your child in your native language or the one you speak at home. Help your child learn to sit still and listen quietly.

2. Have lots of conversation with your child every day. Children learn to use language by experiencing language.

3. Provide opportunities for your child to ask and answer questions. Follow your child's lead and natural curiosity.

4. Take any opportunity to count objects together out loud and point out letters, then sounds.

5. Help your child learn to write his or her name correctly with lower- and uppercase letters.

6. Expose your child daily to songs, rhymes and music.

6. ii) Body Skills

Help your child to learn how to use tools they will use in school — like crayons, pencils, safety scissors and glue. Teach some simple motor skills like balancing on the foot and hopping. Make these simple teachings interesting and fun by playing games. Teach your child to button and zip their clothing.

6. iii) Independence Skills

- Encourage your child to be increasingly responsible and independent about grooming, getting dressed and cleaning up.

- Teach your child to manage his or her own bathroom needs.

- Have your child used to spending time away from you by visiting with friends and family.

You must NOTICE which hand your child is using and inform the teacher as well.

6. iv) Social Development

Supporting children's developing self-concept and sense of positive self-esteem is an important task for parents and teachers of young children. Children can become discouraged quickly if they experience repeated disappointments, failures or frustration.

Preschoolers can engage in cooperative play with other children and form real friendships. In order to develop these social skills, children need catching and guidance to maintain appropriate behavior with others.

The important Social skills comprise:

- Using words instead of being physical when angry.
- Following simple directions.
- Speaking clearly, so that an adult can understand.

- Playing with other children happily.
- Going to the bathroom without help.
- Asking questions about things around them.
- Enjoying having books read aloud to them.
- Telling a tale about some past event.
- Talking using complete sentences.
- Expressing feelings and desires.
- Dressing and eating with minor supervision.
- Using common courtesies (such as please and thank you) and social behavior.
- Socializing with other children successfully and learn about sharing and taking turns.

IMPORTANT

If you notice that your child has difficulty in any of these areas, be sure to let your child's teacher know about this. Though nothing to worry, as most of the children will continue to develop these and other skills throughout the year.

Kidsvill child care

Blk 217

8:30 to 7 AM

lunch at 12 30 AM

sleep at 1 PM

wake up at 2 30 PM

eat at 2 45 PM

lesson at 3 30 PM

dance at 4 30 PM

small wing at 5 30 PM

7.
Learning time management

How to teach time management skills?

Time management helps children feel self-reliant and independent. It's a great way to build their confidence and responsibility. If the time is managed, children feel less stressed while doing their work. They can also manage their time better and will be able to separate study time from play and rest time. This helps them to focus better when they need to study and when to enjoy their playtime. In order to successfully help kids with time management, make it more fun.

The child's effort should always be praised and rewarded. It keeps them motivated to continue working on organizing themselves. You can try some nice encouraging words and tell them that they earned extra time for play.

Do not keep many expectations. Learning to manage time for children is a long and complex process. Support and help your child to manage their time. Use different activities, games and storybooks to help your child learn time management.

Time Management for Kids of 3-4 years of Age

Most children in this age group (ages 3-4) do not have much understanding of time. Therefore, it is best to start making them understand the daily routines. By following daily routine, keeping in mind the duration of time, they will gain an understanding of time management.

At this age, kids bloom on regularity and expectedness, which helps in their cognitive and emotional development.

Here are some ideas on how to make them understand about time and its management.

1. Start a daily routine

Organize your child's daily routine with regular meal time, nap time, free time, play time and tidy-up time. A proper routine helps young kids feel confident and understand what they have to do next. It also helps children understand the importance of time. Set timings for everything like getting ready for school, meals, school homework and going to bed. Fix regular amounts of time for homework, recreation, and naps.

Create colorful timetables with names and pictures of important activities. Pictures are really helpful when it comes to applying daily routines and time management strategies to preschoolers and scholars.

2. Teach your child to keep everything in place

Let's start by teaching them to keep their room and desk in order. They are the important time management aspects. Even awell-prepared timetable can be spoiled by wasting time for looking a lost pencil or notebook. Colorful desk organizers will help keep your child's school articles in place and ready to use all the time. It will help them keep their things in a proper and more organized way.

3. Color coded To-Do List and Visual Time Table

Small children of this age cannot read or write, so whatever they can visualize is the best for them. You can use visual aids and pictures to help visually represent daily activities. Visual timetables with pictures on them, like a sun for wake-up time, a plate for meals, a bed for bedtime, or toys for play time and so on. This can make it simpler and easier for young children to grasp their daily routine. Try putting together a colorful To-Do List with daily, weekly or monthly duties. If your child is more of a tech fan rather than an artsy soul, try one of many applications designed to help kids visualize task lists.

5. Teach value of time

You can teach them the value of time by just playing with them and keeping the time in mind. Also making them understand how long does it take to tidy up the room, doing number work, etc. Effective planning can be done only if we keep the estimated time in mind. Children develop the sense of time around 6 years of age. It's not easy for them to understand "before" and "after". But surely, you can support learning by helping them to know, how to estimate time by using an hourglass, stopwatch or clockwise movements.

6. Activities in small steps

Activities for children should not be more than 15 minutes in duration. Any activity taking longer than an hour, can be divided into smaller stages. It is very important to maintain the child's concentration and motivation. The maximum attention span of a child is around 2-3 minutes multiplied by the child's current age. The maximum concentration time for a five-year old child is about 15 minutes. Hence, all the activities should be planned keeping this in mind to achieve the required outcome.

7. Playtime

Include the concept of time into play activities. Use colourful visual timers for short tasks or games, and explain the passage of time with simple language. For example, say let's play for ten minutes, and after that it will be time to tidy up. This helps children start identifying the duration of activities.

Implementing these practices into daily routines will inculcate time awareness and management skills that will develop along with your child.

Time Management for Children (5 to 7 Year Olds)

As children grow up till the age of 5-7, they are ready for more organized routines. Till this time, they are already in kindergarten to grade 1. They can read and write and begin to understand time in a more concrete and predictable way.

Building upon the simple routines mentioned above, parents and teachers can introduce additional tools and ideas to help children manage their time effectively.

Clocks and Timers:

Children should be introduced to clocks and timers to help them understand time intervals. Use a visual countdown timer for activities like reading or playing, and show them how to read a clock to know when it's time to changeover between tasks.

Setting Time for Specific Activities:

Make a daily timetable that has fixed times for all activities such as homework, playtime, lunch time and bedtime. Having a regular routine helps children know what to expect and eases the struggle with changeovers.

Teaching Task Completion:

It is of utmost importance to teach children to finish the task in hand first before starting a new one. Clear and simple instructions should be used. Always praise your child for completing their tasks. This helps them build focus and discipline, which are the two important aspects of effective time management.

By introducing these structured time management techniques, you help your children develop a more refined understanding of time and the early discipline needed to begin managing it effectively.

8.
Reading Readiness

Barbara Bush, the first lady of the United States, as the wife of President George Bush said, "The home is the child's first school, the parent is the child's first teacher, and reading is the child's first subject."

Isn't this a beautiful thought? She was the founder of the Barbara Bush Foundation for Family Literacy.

So first, let's understand the importance of reading and the role of parental involvement in helping children to learn to read. This information is useful for parents, caregivers and teachers.

Make sure that your home has lots of reading materials that are age appropriate for your child. You can keep books, magazines and newspapers in the house.

By using a few simple tactics, it will make a substantial difference in helping children develop into good readers and writers. Allow children to read aloud, provide print materials, and encourage a positive approach about reading and writing. In this way you can have a powerful impact on children's learning and literacy.

Readiness activities provide young children with the richest learning experiences in a stimulating atmosphere for problem solving, creative thinking and overall development. They also help children to get acquainted with the teacher and motivate them.

Reading Readiness or Pre - Reading Activities

- Reading Readiness Activities should focus upon the development of favorable attitudes towards reading as a useful tool.

- Opportunities to handle storybooks, magazines, listening and telling stories, and different sounds in the environment should be given importance.

- Success in reading depends upon how much time and opportunity the child gets to explore, experience, hear and ask.

- The child needs a variety of material, worksheets and picture story books.

- These activities should be according to individual need.

TIPS

- Identify beginning letter sounds.
- Recognize upper- and lower-case letter names.
- Recognize and make rhyming words.
- Identify and produce groups of words that begin with the same sound (alliteration) (ex: cat, car, catch).
- Segment syllables in spoken words. (ex: pa – per)
- Recognize spacing between the words.
- Identify the front cover, back cover, and title of a book.
- Read basic sight words (ex: the, to, and, in, etc).
- Develop vocabulary for new, unknown words.

- Ask and answer questions in order to seek help, get information, or clarify something that is not understood.
- Follow two step directions (ex: Please put your shoes on and get your backpack).

The Three Essential Components of Reading Are:

1. Phonic Awareness
2. Phonics
3. Reading Flue

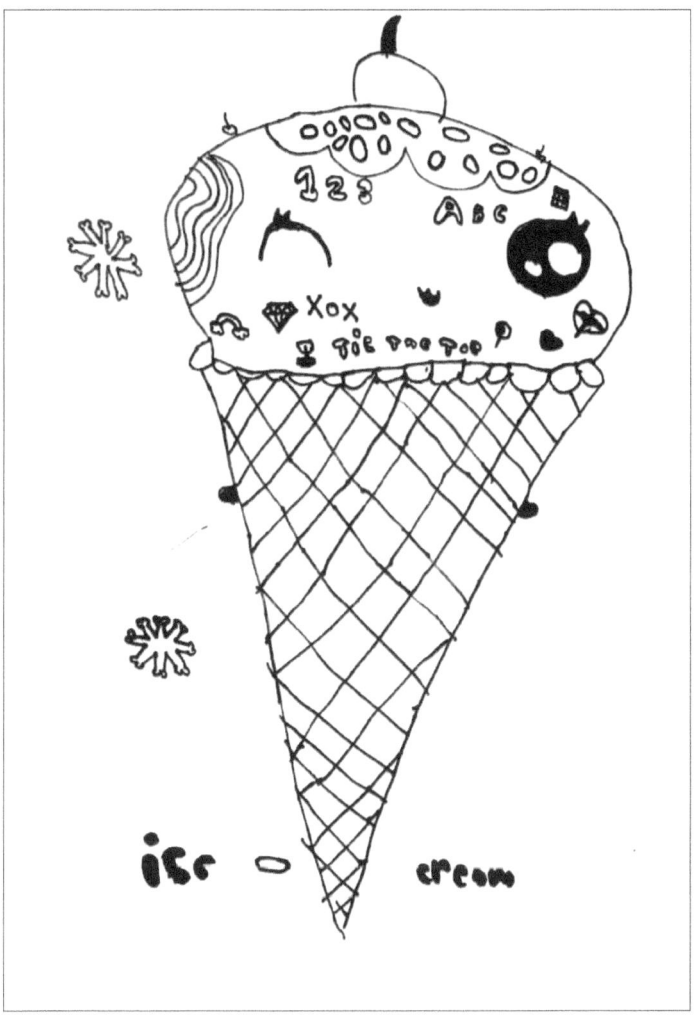

9.
Math Readiness

Math's concepts can be a part of your child's daily experiences. Children, categorizing, comparing, ordering, numbering and counting. In kindergarten, your child will learn basic math skills, concepts, and problem solving.

The development of number concepts. It is about classifying, ordering, counting, and time. They are directly related to children's ability to complete mathematical tasks throughout their school years and the rest of their lives. Mathematics is experienced in day-to-day life and can be implemented in a playful method. It is important to help your child feel confident in dealing with number work.

- Observe page numbers
- Compare sizes: big, small, middle-sized
- Observe position in space: up/down, over/under, in/out, beside/between
- Use number word in order: first, second, third

Children will learn numbers and number concepts. They will be able to use addition and subtraction, identify, and work with shapes.

Asking Hots Questions, can facilitate math readiness and make it fun:

How Questions

- Numbers of letters in a word

- Number of words in a line
- Number of words in a sentence
- How many times a word is written in a page?
- Number of letters in their name
- Let your children set the dining table
- Number of forks you need keeping in mind the members of the family
- Number of plates on the table
- Number of spoons you need with the forks
- Provide opportunities to put away the groceries and keep counting them.
- Provide opportunities to compare objects: color of socks, size of food containers, etc.
- Set up a routine or sequence for personal care.
- Provide objects or toys for play.

IMPORTANT: Here you can see that by following this, we are making Cross Curricular Links with other subjects, which is very important. It opens the mind and their creative thinking.

10.
Science readiness

As children grow up and get mature, they naturally become more curious about their environment and begin to interact with their surroundings. This is the best time to introduce them to science. Rich sensory experiences (seeing, tasting, touching, hearing, and smiling) can help children become ever more observant and curious about the world around them.

Experience and research show that young children become excited about science when given the chance to "do" science.

Hands-on science experiments, along with conversations about what is happening, are the most useful for developing children's science capabilities. They engage in science problem solving and begin to understand the "how" and "what" of things.

Exploring the characteristics of objects and living things can help children learn how to classify or group things based on their characteristics. These experiences go beyond improving science skills to improving reading skills, language skills, creativity and attitudes towards science. Many skills that help your children succeed in science also help in everyday life.

It is important to address and satisfy children's curiosity. If you cannot answer some of their questions, that's okay. No one has all the answers! The answers to their queries should be short, clear and crisp.

Science Skills Include:

- Observing what is happening
- Predicting what might happen
- Testing predictions under controlled conditions
- Understanding the observations

Science in the Home and Neighborhood

There are many activities you can do with your children to help them develop skills related to science.

How can you help at home?

- Introduce your children to stimulating environments - oceans, parks, airports, kitchens and backyards offer chances for observing and discussing science.

- Become involved in your children's science interests. Identify aspects of science that your child enjoys.

- If dinosaurs intrigue him, read dinosaurs books, visit museums, and watch a video about dinosaurs.

- Seize the teachable moments. If your child shows an interest in flowers, talk about it. You can follow up by planting flowers and watching them grow.

- Provide hands-on experience. Give children the chance "to do" science. Activities should challenge but not overly frustrate.

- Bridge from the media, using what your children see on television to open science opportunities.

- Set aside time for discussion.

- Encourage your children to keep asking questions, just like scientists.
- Let your child know you don't have all the answers, and together try to find them.

11
Role of Art, Music and Physical Education

Arts and Music are the two sides of the same coin and go hand in hand with physical education in the development of children

Arts and stories are great avenues for introducing young students to social sciences (sometimes called social studies). Art activities done along with music provide an important learning experience for children. They explore creativity and self-expression. The learning becomes very interesting and engaging.

These projects will also help children develop small muscle groups as well as gain knowledge. Social skills, life sharing and cooperation, responding positively and making decisions are some of them.

How can you help at home?

- Teach your children songs with actions.
- Listen to music and sing along.
- Play catch with your child while playing music.
- Let them listen to music and imagine a situation, and then draw it.
- Color together and give your child access to art materials or craft activities.

- Share stories that have characters from other cultures or historical periods.
- Look at maps together and talk about other parts of the world.

"We cannot always build the future for our youth, but we can build our youth for the future"

Franklin D. Roosevelt

Meaning, we have to nurture our coming generation in such a way so that they can very smoothly sail into the boat of future.

For this smooth sailing there are some essential building blocks or we can say the core points for the smooth transition to future life.

12.
Important building blocks

- 12 (i) Raising A Confident Child
- 12 (ii) Effective Discipline Strategies
- 12 (iii) Spanking Will Not Help

12 (i) Raising a Confident Child

How to Raise a Confident and Happy Child?

Assurance is one of the greatest gifts a parent can give to their child. The child should know loud and clear that you are always there for him. This builds in confidence in them. Lack of confidence can hold them back from coming out and shine. This lack can prevent them from having a bright future.

Self-confidence comes from a sense of ability. A confident child needs a positive and genuine opinion of his or her abilities. This comes out of achievements, great and small. This confidence can be developed by your encouraging words, particularly when the child has shown special efforts for the specific work.

The two enemies of confidence are **discouragement** and **fear**. So, as a parent, it's your job to encourage and support your child as they try to tackle difficult tasks.

Here are some more tips for raising a confident child:

1. The effort put in by the child must get appreciation

Have you heard of the DOT day? It is one of the finest examples of encouragement. While growing up, the journey is more important than the final destination. So, whether your child wins or not, we must applaud their effort. They should never feel embarrassed for trying again.

2. Practice makes the man perfect

The child should be encouraged to practice whatever they're interested in and should not put too much pressure on them. There are many people who started practicing very young and became great people and were very successful.

3. Kids should figure out the problems independently

Let your child do the hard work and figure out problems; otherwise, they will never be able to do things on their own. It is always better that your child gets a few B's and C's rather than straight A's as long as they are learning how to solve the problems and do the work. In the long run, this trial and error will help them gain confidence.

4. Kids should act their age

Kids are small, and we should not expect them to act as us. They will lose confidence if we pressurise them to behave older than their age. They will be mature before they should be, and it is not healthy for their development.

5. Child's curiosity should be encouraged

Children are used to asking a lot of questions out of curiosity, and we tend to get tired or irritated. We should encourage them and be patient while answering their queries. Asking questions is a helpful exercise for a child's development. If a child wants to know the 'how' 'when' 'what' then this shows they understand, that there are many things they need to know. Hence, it makes them curious. The children who grow up in the families who encourage 'curious questions' have an edge over the rest of other children in class or neighbourhood. This is all because they've had practice taking in information from their parents. In other words, they know how to learn better and faster.

6. Children love challenges so give them

Believe in them and give your child small goals to reach a big accomplishment. As quoted by a famous psychologist, **Pickhardt,** "Parents can nurture confidence by increasing responsibilities that must be met."

7. Do not judge your child

Instead of finding faults, just appreciate. Children get discouraged when they are criticised and their efforts not recognised. Giving suggestions is fine – but **remember**, refrain from giving them ***negative remarks***. If your child is scared to fail because they worry you'll be angry or disappointed, they'll never try new things. So never get angry, even if they make a mistake or have done it wrongly. At least they tried and made an effort to do that work.

8. Treat mistakes as opportunity for learning

Making mistakes is healthy because with every mistake they are learning. You, as a parent should treat their mistakes as an opportunity to learn and grow. Don't be overprotective of your child. Allow them to mess up every now and then and help them understand how they can improve the task next time. That is how their failures will lead them to success.

9. If they see you as their idol then be one

A child always sees his/her parents as their idol until they grow up. So, it's time for you to set an example for them as to how you think, behave and react. Take it as an opportunity for setting a good example for them. It will help them gain more confident.

10. They should not know about your fears

If children see their parents worried, they get anxious and in turn, lack confidence. They feel insecure and stressful.

11. Praise them when they deal with difficulty

Life is not easy and fair. Children will have to learn by involving and experimenting themselves. While doing so, they will make mistakes and might come across hardships. It is your duty as parents to point out how lasting these challenges will be.

We as adults have to be their constant guides and teach them resilience. It's important to remind your child time and again that every road that leads to victory has to pass ups and downs.

12. Do not make them too dependent by offering lot of assistance

Giving too much assistance and too soon can reduce the child's ability for self-help. When children learn on their own by using their thinking skills, and creative skills, then they learn faster. It might take time but when they do something themselves, they are more confident, happy and satisfied.

13. Appreciate their courage to try something new

Whether it's trying out for the travel basketball team or going on their first roller coaster, parents should praise their kids for trying new things. I suggest saying simple words as, "Come on! You can do this!" A feeling of natural relief comes if it comes from the parents. The willingness and a can-do approach can help your child for the whole life. We have to make our children courageous to dare new things and learn by experimenting on their own.

14. Learning should be made rejoiceful

The journey and the joy of learning something are of utmost importance. Winning or losing doesn't matter; what matters is the effort that your child has put in. *The willingness to attempt something and to work hard for it, is the real achievement. We should never make him feel embarrassed for trying.*

15. They should learn to live in real life and not waste all time in internet

There should be restrictions on computer time. They should be encouraged to get involved with the people around them. Though the virtual world is also important to gain knowledge, but interacting and spending time with other children and people brings confidence. They learn the art of empathy and gratitude, which are very important aspects of being a human being.

16. You should be the authority, but must give them free hand too

Children should be given free hands to work. This means that when they get too many instructions and strict warnings, they tend to lose interest. They are too scared to try new things and are not confident enough to face results. Therefore, parents have to be firm, not very strict.

12 (ii) Tips for Effective Discipline

1. Most importantly, your child should know that you love him

When a child is born, what is the first emotion that we show and give? It's LOVE. Only then does the child respond, isn't it? So, you must give lots of love and attention to your child. This helps in developing trust for you in child. He needs to feel accepted and loved, beginning with the family and extending to other groups such as friends, schoolmates, sports teams, and the community. If you yell, ignore or make some other parenting mistake, give your child a hug and tell her you're sorry and you love her. Unconditional love builds a strong foundation for confidence.

2. Always Praise where needed

It's important to give your child praise and positive feedback because children—especially young ones—measure their worth and achievements by what you think. But be realistic in your praise. If a child fails at something or shows no talent at a particular skill, praise the effort, but don't unrealistically praise the results. Reassure your child that it's OK not to be able to do everything perfectly. Tell him that some things take repeated effort and practice—and sometimes it's OK to move on after you've given your best effort.

3. Always guide and help your child to set genuine goals

When your child is starting out in soccer, its fine for her to think she'll eventually be on the Olympic team. But if she fails to make the varsity team in high school and still thinks she's an Olympic-calibre player, then she needs to focus on more realistic goals. Guide your child to set reasonable goals to help avoid feelings of failure. If the goal is a stretch, discuss some reachable short-term steps along the path.

4. <u>Practice self-love and positive self-talk to teach your kids</u>

You must love yourself before you can teach your child to love himself or herself. You can model this behaviour by rewarding and praising yourself when you do well. Whether you run a marathon, get a promotion at work or throw a successful dinner party, celebrate your successes with your children. Talk about the skills, talents and efforts needed for you to achieve those accomplishments. In the same conversation, you can remind your child of the skills he or she possesses and how they can be developed and used.

5. <u>You must teach resilience</u>

It is not necessary that a person succeed in everything that he does. There might be failures, setbacks, criticism and discomfort. We should use these obstacles as learning experiences rather than failures or disappointments. There is an old saying, "Try, try again." While teaching kids, do not give up, have patience. At the same time, it is very important to understand your child's feelings and not just say, "Cheer up, it's okay." This supports children to overcome the unsuccessful effort. They learn to trust their feelings and feel comfortable sharing them. Children will understand that setbacks are a normal part of life and can be managed. For example, if your child does not perform well in a test, don't ever discourage or say bad words. Instead, talk about how he can do better next time and help him in where he needs more effort.

6. Instill independence and exploration

Children with confidence are willing to try new things without any fear of setbacks. As far as small kids are concerned, you will need to keep an eye on them. Make them practice such situations by making one. Let the child do things on his own and handle the situation but make sure the situation is safe. Like, you can show how to cook without fire. Make a simple sandwich and then let him try it on his own; do not interfere or help. Inspire their investigation, whether it's a trip to a new park or new foods at lunchtime. School picnics and outings, new hobbies, vacations and trips with teammates or schoolmates can all expand your child's horizons and build confidence in their ability to handle new situations.

7. Sports and other physical activities should be encouraged

Sport plays an important role in building confidence in both girls and boys. It helps them to improve and achieve goals. The other advantages of sports are: children learn to recognize their strong and weak points. They also learn to handle defeat and setbacks. They grow their circle of friends and learn teamwork. Another confidence-enhancing advantage: they stay fit and learn to respect their bodies. Nowadays, obesity is common among children. Hence it is very important, to take care of their bodies. Try to find a physical activity that he or she enjoys, whether it's dance, martial arts, biking or hiking.

8. Always support your child while achieving their interests

We all excel at something or the other, and its great when your child realizes that **something**. As a parent, respect and encourage your child's interests—even if you are not interested in them. Praise your child when they achieve something in their growing hobbies. If your child's talent is playing a violin, then support his interest, as long as it doesn't get in the way of responsibilities like schoolwork. Also, this does not mean you leave your child to just play violin. You will have to make him learn to manage both hobbies and education. Once he masters the management, he will succeed, and he will take pride in his accomplishments.

9. Set rules and be logical

Children are more independent when they recognize who is giving the orders and what to expect. Even if your child thinks that the rules you implemented are very strict, he will still be confident in what he can do and what he cannot do. Every home has different rules, and they will change with time according to your child's age. In setting your household rules, make sure that they are loud and clear on what is important in your family. Understanding and then following the rules gives children a sense of safety and confidence. As children mature and get older, they will have more rules and responsibilities different from the previous ones, but it's important to remember that first you are the parent and then a best friend. If your child feels peer pressure someday, then he should have the confidence to say, "I am strong enough to deal."

10. Teach bonding skills

Confidence in relationships is key to your child's self-confidence. The most important early relationship is the parent-child relationship. As your child's social circle expands, you should help him see how his actions and comments affect other people. Help your child to learn to maintain his confidence when someone else's actions affect him. As a parent, it's not your duty to resolve every situation, but rather to educate your child on the empathy, kindness, self-assertiveness, and confidence to handle the ups and downs of our relationship.

12 (iii) Spanking will not help, instead can do irreparable loss

"To lose patience is to lose the battle." – Mahatma Gandhi

What is actually spanking? Spanking is slapping the child on the buttocks with bare hands. Spanking is not the solution to change your child's behaviour or habits. Though it is one of the most commonly discussed parenting topics. The paediatricians and parenting professionals don't endorse spanking, but most parents around the world admit to spanking their kids.

For most of the parents, they feel spanking is the fastest, easiest and most effective way to change a child's behaviour. But the research done has confirmed that corporal punishment has long-term consequences for kids.

There are many ways in place of spanking. I have mentioned some ways to discipline your child without using physical punishment.

1. Teach them the Time-Out Way

Spanking children for misbehaviour (especially violent behaviour) makes the child confused. Your child will wonder why it's OK for you to hit him but not OK for him to hit his sister. Why?

Placing a child in **time-out that is taking a** break can be a much better substitute. When done properly, time-out teaches children how to calm themselves down, which in turn will be an important and useful life skill.

But for time-out to be effective, kids need to have plenty of time with their parents. Then, when they're removed from that particular situation, the lack of attention will be uncomfortable, and that discomfort could remind them to behave better in the future.

2. <u>Take Away Liberties</u>

Although a spanking stings for a minute or two, liberty can hurt for a longer duration and will be more effective. Take away the TV, video games, his favourite toy or a fun activity for the day and he'll remember not to repeat that mistake.

Make it clear when the liberties can be earned back. Usually, 24 hours is long enough to teach your child to learn from his mistake.

So, you might say, "You've lost the TV time for the whole day, but you can earn it back again the next day by picking up your toys as soon as I ask you".

3. <u>Overlook Slight Misbehaviour</u>

Slight misbehaviour can be ignored and it can be more effective than spanking. This definitely does not mean that you should overlook what your child is doing, especially something dangerous or inappropriate. But the attention-seeking behaviour should be ignored.

When your child tries to get attention by **whining** or complaining, don't give it to him. Do not respond and pretend you have not heard him say anything.

Only, when he asks nicely or he behaves, give your attention to him. Over time, he'll learn that polite behaviour is the best way to get his needs met.

4. <u>Awareness of sensible fines</u>

Fines are a great way to help kids who are struggling with specific behaviour problems.

For example, if your child does not want to eat his food, don't let him have an evening snack. If he refuses to tidy up his toys mess, then do not allow him to play with them for the rest of the day.

Linking the consequence directly to the behaviour problem helps kids see that their choices have direct consequences. Allow for Natural Penalties

5. <u>Natural Penalties</u>

Children need to learn from their own mistakes and we should help them do this.

For example, if your child says he's not going to wear a jacket, let him go outside and get cold—as long as it's safe to do so.

Use natural consequences when you think your child will learn from his own mistake. Keep an eye on the situation to safeguard that your child will not experience any real threat.

6. <u>Reward Good Behaviour</u>

Instead of spanking a child for misbehaviour, **reward him for good behaviour.** For example, if your child does not get along with his siblings, then set up an incentive system to encourage him to get along better with them.

Giving an incentive to behave can work very well and reverse the misbehaviour. Rewards and incentives help kids to focus on what they need to do and improve to earn privileges. This also distracts them from misbehaving.

7. Always Praise Good Behaviour

Praise the good behaviour of your child, if he is being good. For example, when your child is behaving and playing nicely with his siblings, point it out. Be vocal about it. Say, "wow! It's so nice. You are doing such a great job sharing and taking turns today. Let's do Hi Five!"

Give more attention and **praise** to the children, who are following the rules and behaving well. Then, when the other children begin to behave, give them also praise and attention as well.

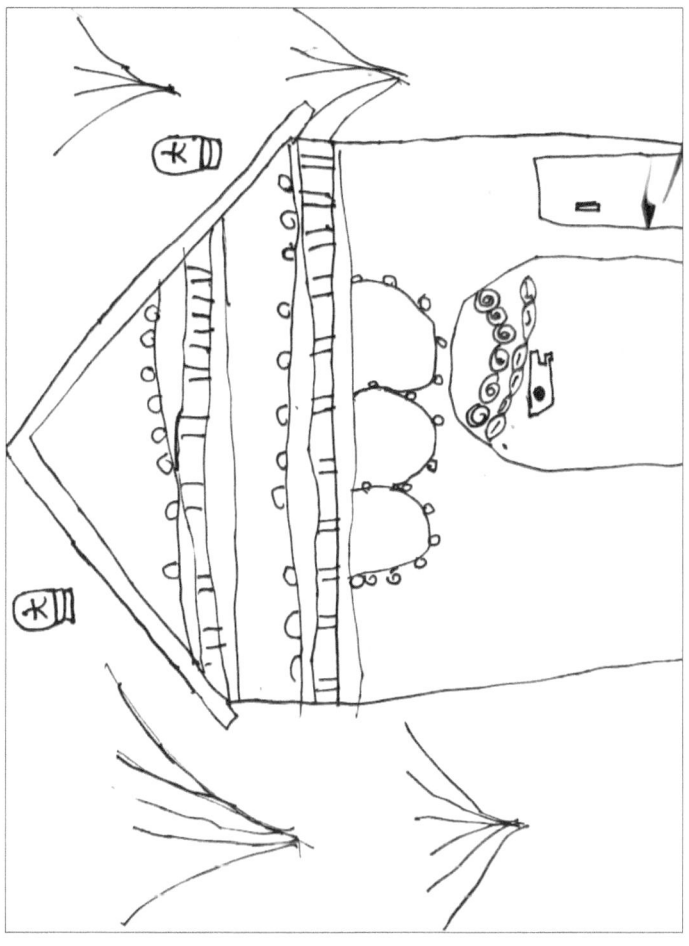

Important building blocks

13.
Conversations that make difference

- 13. (i) Building a Bond with your child
- 13. (ii) Nature Walks
- 13. (iii) Inculcating Moral Values in your child
- 13. (iv) Understanding your child's preferred style

"A father's goodness is higher than the mountain, a mother's goodness deeper than the sea."

-Japanese Proverb

This Japanese proverb says it all. Both the father and mother are the pillars of strength for their children. Their love is so great and pure which has no boundaries and no heights. This deep love plays the vital role in the overall development of a child.

13 (i) Building a Bond with Your Child

Life is so busy. Did we remember to buy milk? Where are my school shoes? Who let the dog inside with those muddy paws? Sometimes it feels like we need more hours in the day just to get through the basics. We need quality time to read, draw, play and spend time with our kids. But the research shows that it's those intimate moments reading a book, or on a walk, talking and engaging face-to-face, that help build a strong bond between parent and child.

It's that connection that will be a child's most powerful experience of love and build the foundations and predictors of their future success. So here are some ideas for how to make an unbreakable connection with your child.

1. Art

Exploring art with your child, watching their little brains absorb all the colorful details of a painting or a picture book – is a precious way to spark the connection. Young children often find it hard to articulate complex emotions, but art offers a visual focus that frees us to be creative and open up about our feelings. A child who experiences that secure early attachment grows up to be an emotionally capable and resilient adult rather than an anxious person who doesn't cope well with life's setbacks.

2. Books are a great source of bonding

Earlier, when there was no other source of entertainment, parents and grandparents used to tell stories of life experiences, animals, birds, families and many more. Children used to enjoy that time and used to look forward to it. It had a great impact on them and played a vital role in their development. It was the only source of bonding between parents and children.

Reading books and storytelling with your child helps brain development and thinking skills. It helps your child understand the language and emotions and also makes your relationship stronger. Books generate deep emotional bonds between kids and adults when they read together. Books are very interactive and they compel the kids to think.

They are the best friends for kids. They develop and cultivate kids' thoughts, expanding their social world. Picture books introduce young children to art and literature. Books inform our imaginations, inspiring creativity.

Children are able to experience the world through the books before they have to go out into it. This means that they give kids a chance to experience something in their thoughts before it happens to them in real life. They help prepare kids for their next stage of maturity.

3. Ritual

A ritual can be a beautiful way to bond with your family and create a sense of belonging. It could be something as simple as playing board games on a Sunday night, or planting bulbs to come up in the spring or praying together. It just has to have meaning that ties you together.

For children at primary school, it could be a scrapbooking project that you do together – reflecting back on the important events and milestones of the year in a visual collage or maybe it's a 'no phones' rule when you're having dinner, so you can give each other your full attention. Whatever traditions you choose, the point is to enjoy a shared experience, something you do together to cement your bond – so that as your children grow up, no matter what happens, they will always feel tied to you – like a trusted anchor, grounding them with strong and stable support.

13 (ii) Nature Walks

It is always good to be near nature. Nature plays a vital role in the development of kids and helps them to become more resilient and full of gratitude. Nature helps children to focus better and relieves their stress.

It improves imagination! Nature walks are also a superb way to instill in children a gratitude for the environment and a sense of responsibility for its well-being from an early age. After exploring and learning about the environment, they'll be more motivated to take action to protect the planet Earth as they grow older.

It will be an extremely fun and worthwhile experience taking a nature walk with.

Here are some ideas to make the trips happy and enriching.

1. Location should be child friendly

The location for your nature walk should be appropriate and should be selected keeping in mind the small children. It should be for little ones to enjoy happily.

Try to look for clear paths that allow you to focus on the experience without any difficulty. It can be an easier trail, a community park, or a walk around your neighborhood. The right choice of location is key to a happy nature walk.

2. Pre Nature walk preparations

It is of utmost importance to wear comfortable and strong shoes. Everything that you may need along the way on your nature walk should be kept before you set out. Do remember to bring essentials such as sunscreen, water and some snacks, as you have small children with you and never know when someone might get hungry. A proper first aid kit should be on the priority list in case of a minor injury.

3. Boost Investigation

It's a great opportunity for your children to explore their surroundings. Nature walks are encouraged and let them engage with their environment by feeling and touching different textures and observing various plants and animals. Let them carry the magnifying glass, letting them take a closer look at their discoveries. You can also carry binoculars so that from time to time they can have a look at the things far away and explore the experience.

Some interesting activities can be included in the nature walks to make them more exciting and interesting.

How about taking your children's nature walk experience to an another level? Keep them well engaged with an exciting bingo card activity highlighting different plants, animals, and other natural wonders they may come across on their adventure.

These bingo cards can be printed and let each child mark off each item with a highlighter as they spot it during the nature walk. Keep the card handy and continue to play the game on future walks until every square has been marked off. When they complete the card, celebrate their achievement together. You could even reward them with a small treat or surprise.

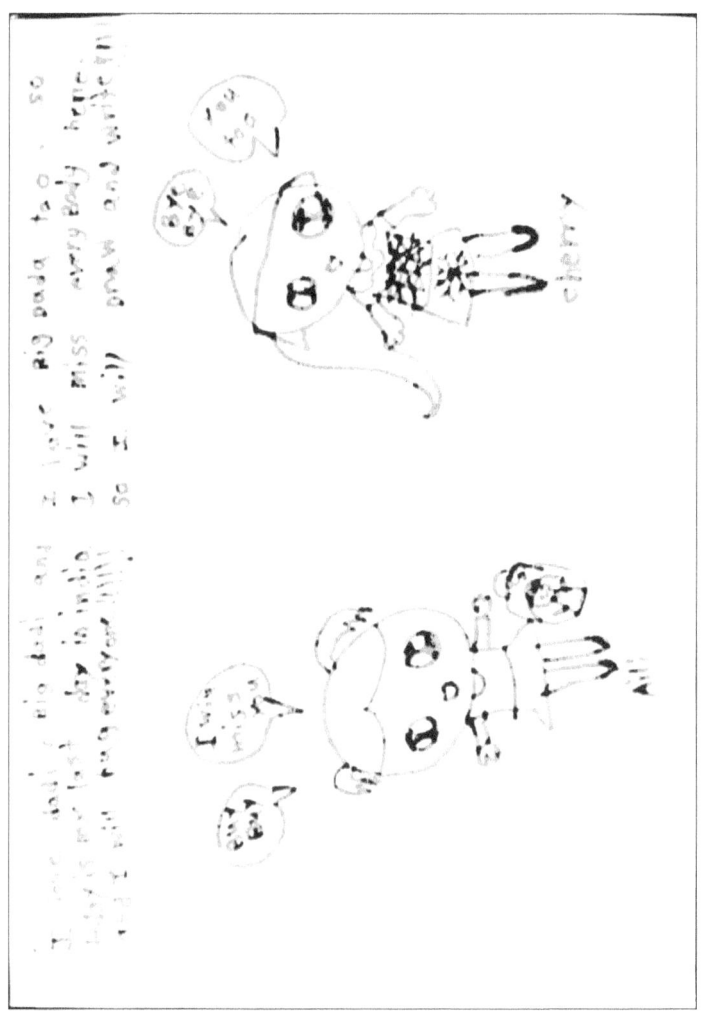

13. (iii) Inculcating Moral Values in your Child

Instilling the difference between right and wrong, good and evil, and appropriate and inappropriate behavior is quite challenging. It is very important to make the child understand the importance of early spiritual training. This can be done by reading them the spiritual books like the Bible, Ramayana, Panchatantra and all other moral stories. But the challenge lies in teaching practical moral values.

It's an ongoing process. Faith in God is experienced with everyday life experiences and influences attitudes and decisions.

We have to teach them respect for others and outside the family, irrespective of age, race, sex, appearance or behavior. Respect for the property and belongings of others.

We have a big responsibility to make our children understand that real happiness does not come from material things. We as parents need to set an example by following the same rules so that they grow up and develop by experiencing them with us.

A pledge for honesty and truthfulness, along with a constant habit of telling the truth should be inculcated.

Self-control, self-discipline and an understanding of the importance of gratitude while working toward future goals should be well taught at home and in school as well. It is the duty of parents and teachers to help develop these in children.

We must apply all these in our day-to-day life because children learn what they live.

The Importance of moral values for kids

Story telling is one of the best ways to instill moral values in our kids. Kids like to hear stories and can very well relate to them. Once upon a time, when I was a little girl, my mother used to read one story every night from the 'Panchatantra tales'. There were so many to name some – Chandama, Nandan, Amarchitra Katha, Champak, etc. They were so interacting and interesting that I used to wait for the next night eagerly. Each story had a moral in it. The next day, my mother used to ask so many 'hots questions' regarding that story and the moral I learnt from it. It so beautifully and easily got merged in my mind and thoughts, that till today I remember each word of it. My parents made sure that they gifted me 'Books' on my birthday. This same tradition I followed for my children and I am so proud of my children to follow the same for Alysaa and Axel, my loving grandchildren.

Narrate stories and fables

This is how parents can raise morally intelligent children with the help of stories that impart moral values to them. They are rich resources to teach values. They can be bedtime stories or simple stories in the afternoons and evenings. Aesop's fables, stories from the scriptures - all these are full of moral tales. Your child will connect more to stories than any other form of teaching.

Hence why it is important to inculcate values in kids.

Expose your children to important life lessons early in life. Instilling good morals helps them understand the difference between right and wrong. They develop the right qualities and habits that lead them to success. It also helps them to counter the negative influences in society by becoming better citizens..

Schools also inculcate values in numerous ways like the morning assembly, class assembly, circle time, posters and quotes, and thought for the day. Besides this training children to be polite, respectful, punctual, etc. But it is the home where the values are imbibed most instinctively and effectively.

To know more about how you can do this, here are some ideas on how to instill values and build their character.

Always practice what you preach

Always be very clear about your own understanding of what is right and what is wrong. Set the right morals for your child. Make sure that you do what you want them to do. If you do not endorse values and moralities in your day-to-day life but want your child to do so, you would be sending a confusing message to your children. We as parents should always remember that parental influence is very strong on a child when it comes to morals and values.

Explain them, what are values?

You can explain the values to your children only if you also follow them religiously. You should have your values evidently in place otherwise, you will not be able to explain them or pass them on to your child. The value system should be properly explained in order to inculcate it in your kids. Your child will be influenced by the beliefs you stand for and use.

Moral growth

Along with physical development - mental, emotional, and social development are also very important. Parents need to pay attention on all these areas. However, the most important aspect of your child's development is the molding of their character. This can be achieved only, if you highlight and stay dedicated to the moral development of your child.

Make sure learning happens everyday

All that happens and all that you say in everyday life at home should be used to inculcate values in your child. The learning should happen all the time- while playing, eating, working, and other chores. These day-to-day teachings are the best at teaching him the moral values. Children develop empathy and gratitude this way. If you see someone is honest or kind at once point it out to your child, so that then and there they can understand the value of honesty. The same is if someone doesn't have any respect for values, explain it to your child and how it impacts. Learning becomes easy and understandable while playing. Playtime should be used to impart these lessons. Such practical learning will embed in your child, helping him to raise with a strong intellect of values. Actually, you can touch every teachable moment possible to impart values to your child.

Always appreciate good behavior

Always remember you must acknowledge when good values are shown by your child. Whenever you notice your child's actions or words reflecting good values, appreciate it. Appreciate your child when his behaviour is good. Remember, positive words always help. This appreciation will help emphasize the practice of their good values. Remember not to punish your child if any wrong deed is done by him. Talk to him about it nicely and explain to him how and why it is wrong to behave in that way. Make sure you establish a connection with your child while talking to him about his unacceptable behaviour. This will reassure him to behave in a good manner. Imparting a clear sense of right and wrong,

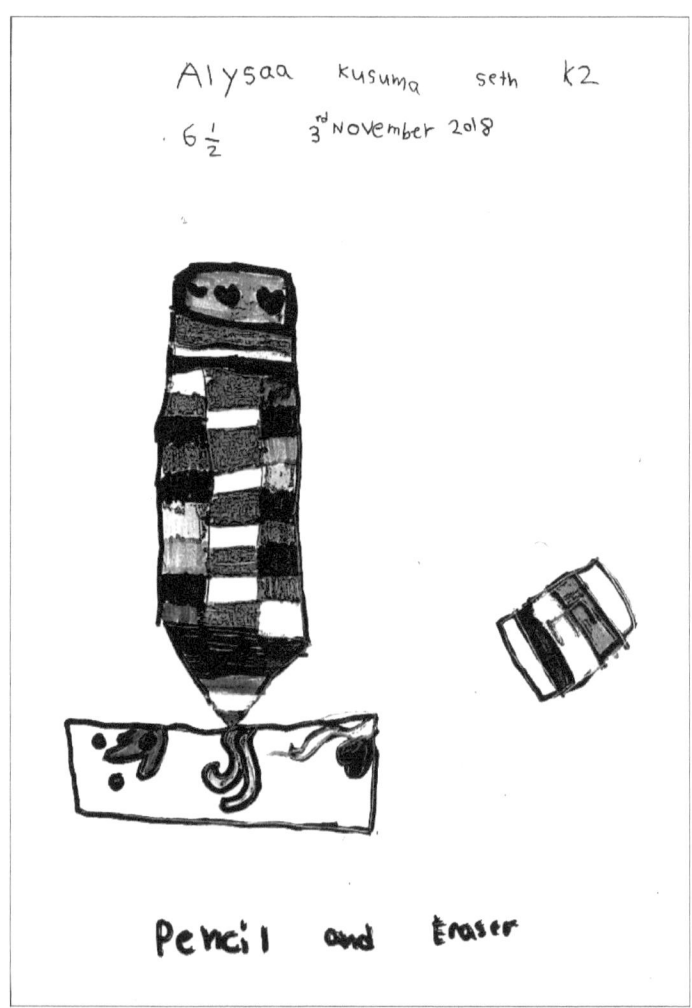

appreciating good behaviour, teaching effective problem-solving and conflict-resolution, and being a good role model for your child are some ways to do it.

'To educate a man in mind and not in morals is a menace to society,' said the former American President Theodore Roosevelt. As parents, let us pledge to educate our children on values, principles, and ethics. And let us begin early, even as they are at the threshold of formal education - the preschool stage.

13. (iv) Try to understand your child's preferred learning style

We must remember that each child is unique and a beautiful creation of God. Every child has different capabilities and styles of learning.

It is very important to understand how your child learns. It is perhaps one of the most important tasks a parent can undergo while they are at home. Another is understanding how to make available the opportunities for learning by using these identified learning methods.

- How a child thinks and the way they sense and perceive their surroundings often affects the way they learn. The connections to memory are also associated with our senses and observations, creating a complex and often individualized process of learning.

- Different personalities focus on attention, emotion, and values. Understanding these differences allows you to calculate the way your child might react and feel about different situations.

- Social interactions - attitudes, habits, and strategies learners might take toward their work and how they engage with others when they learn. Learners can be independent, dependent, collaborative, competitive, participant or avoidant.

- Interest plays a critical role in learning. When a student is interested in the topics or subjects, they naturally learn and retain information at a higher rate.
- Helping your child develop a variety of interests will naturally increase their level of learning overall.

Many researchers and educators have identified three main types of learning - kinesthetic, visual, and auditory.

Kinesthetic learners

Signs, your child is a kinaesthetic learner

- Aptitude in sports, dance, or other physical activities
- Tendency to fidget while in his/her seat — It's their way; they may need to move while processing information.
- Some may use gestures frequently when speaking or explaining things.
- A love of hands-on activities and play-acting.
- Enjoys writing, drawing, or handwriting exercises.
- Physical development, such as early walking, crawling, or sitting early.
- Sharp hand-eye coordination.

Auditory Learner

Some signs that your child is an aural learner

- Aptitude in music, instruments, or vocal ability

- Tendency to sing along to songs or to create her/his own songs as she/he plays
- Strong verbal ability, especially through repetition of words or phrases they have heard before
- Ability to listen well and follow verbal directions
- A love for talking and discussions
- Sharp ability to notice sounds that others don't recognize
- Perking up when she/he hears music or dialog

Visual Learners

Some signs that your child is a visual learner

- An interest in art: painting, drawing, or crafts
- A strong memory that relays visually-observed information
- A good understanding of maps and sense of direction
- An aptitude for reading and a love of books
- Recognition of people, faces, and places
- A keen interest in observing the world around her/him

14.
It's a big world

- 14 (i) Internet and Online Safety
- 14 (ii) Dealing with Bullying
- 14 (iii) Good Touch Bad Touch

"Kids deserve to be happy, healthy and safe."

14 (i) Internet and Online safety

The internet is a great tool for children to learn, express themselves, and make friends. But it can also expose them to graphic content, predators or dangerous links. Here's how to teach your children about internet safety.

When it comes to online safety, parents play a huge role. It's your job to teach your children how they can protect themselves from the dangers of the internet.

Make sure you discuss internet safety with your children today. Educating your child on online safety will help them grow and be safe in this digital age.

1. Establish rules about using the internet

Having clear rules about internet usage can help make it safer for your child. Make rules about how long they're allowed to be online. Also have rules about what they can and can't do when you're not around. Set the time limit and no matter what, stick to it.

2. Use parental controls

If you aren't around a lot and your child has free access to the internet, make sure to set up parental controls. Parental controls are programs that control your child's internet usage.

For example, it could restrict certain websites and services or cut off the internet connection after a certain time. It could also allow you to view your children's online activities.

3. Keep your computer in a high-traffic area

Another great practice for online safety is to put your family computer in a high-traffic area in your home. That way, you develop a culture of transparency and honesty when using the internet.

4. Block in-app purchases and disable one-click payment options on your devices

Many children play games online. The bad news is that many of these games charge a fee to play or to access parts of the game. It is very important to make your child understand that everything you do is for their good.

5. Protect your computer

It's not enough to just tell your child to be careful of what they download. Always install a strong antivirus program on your child's computer. You'll also need to make sure it's updated regularly.

Depending on how young your child is, you should also take steps to make sure they don't accidentally delete any important data from your computer.

14 (ii) *Dealing with Bullying*

Anecdote *I remember a small incident when, Alysaa, my granddaughter was five years old. One day after coming back from school, she was kind of sad but she didn't say anything, even after asking many times. The next morning, she started complaining about stomach aches and didn't want to go to school. A five-year-old girl who was "cheerful, happy and creative" suddenly appeared gloomy, irritable and angry. This little girl, who loved her grade and used to cry when she had to stay home when sick, seemed to have changed overnight. Her mom used to drop her off at school. When her lunch returned home mostly uneaten each day, her mom assumed that she was spending the lunch period chatting with her friends. Mom wondered about "quick lunches" that her daughter could gulp down while she talked.*

When she started refusing to go to school, her mom started worrying, which is very genuine. Alysaa wasn't talking about it, but her mom was intuitive that something wasn't right. Stomach aches kept her up at night and affected her morning routine. In a matter of days, long and intense breakdowns made it nearly impossible to get Alysaa to the school which she once loved.

My son took her to the doctor but all in vain. Her stomach ache was as it is. Though we were worried also, but somewhere I had the feeling that it was something else. So, her mother talked to her very patiently and found out that some of the classmates were making fun of her and she was sad about it. Therefore, she didn't want to face them in school.

As it turned out, **Alysaa** *was being* **bullied** *at school. At first, it was merely a couple of friends moving on and not always including her. The friends she had since kindergarten made it clear that they were no longer her friends.* **While there weren't any shirt-tearing,** *loud screaming or physical aggression of any kind, there was a solid dose of exclusion.*

Sometimes the signs of bullying are obvious. Physical bullying is dangerous. Parents come to know and can begin to track things that can be seen like missing toys or personal belongings and unexplained bruises are signs that something is wrong. More often, bullying is difficult to spot. Children generally don't come home from school saying, "I'm being frightened every day by other kids and I'm really afraid and sad." They also don't know how to describe it. Parents need to look out for such signs, if they find some changes in the child's behaviour.

Watch for these signs that your child might be dealing with a bully:

- *school refusal*
- *repeated stomach aches, headaches and other physical complaints*
- *agitation and moodiness*
- *sleep disturbance (including nightmares and difficulty falling asleep)*
- *changes in eating habits*
- *bedwetting*
- *looking sad, lonely, and anxious with no known reason*
- *avoiding communications*
- *talking about being alone at school*
- *increased self-blame*
- *feeling helpless or worthless*

- *afraid of riding the bus*
- *sudden change in school performance*

1. **School denial is the first and most important sign of bullying**.

If your child usually enjoys attending school and suddenly doesn't want to go, it's time to consider what might be happening. We need to observe his/her behaviour for some days to know the real reason. Children develop social skills as they grow, and some have more refined skills than others. Hence, it is important to know what to do if you are suspicious that your child is being bullied.

2. **Do not assume on your own**

The most important thing to do is to listen to your child without judgment. Remember not to ask questions like, if he said something to upset them or was the first one to say. This is the most common mistake that the parents make. Just to find out the problem with his peers, the parents start judging their children too early. In this way, their own child becomes the offender, though he is the victim.

Your child needs your unconditional love and support right now.

3. **Comment on changes and watch for nonverbal clues.**

Always observe for clues, if your child isn't talking but you suspect that something is wrong, try to observe their behaviour. The best time to talk to kids is not right before or right after school. The best time is when they are peaceful and are spending time with you while lying down, eating dinner or reading stories. At that time talk to them casually saying, "I noticed that you don't want to play with your friends much anymore; are you still hanging out with them?" gives your child an opening without feeling interrogated.

4. Don't schedule a meeting with the other kid(s).

I've seen a lot in the past that the parents fix meetings with both their child and the other children face-to-face to solve the problem. But they don't understand this ends up being awkward and uncomfortable for both kids and doesn't actually help in resolving the issues.

If the families are known and the kids are having trouble getting along then, it isn't "bullying." In this matter, a family get-together might be useful.

5. Do ask the teacher for help

It's no big secret that a lot of bullying and other mean behaviour occurs on the bus, in the cafeteria and during recess, so your child's teacher might not be aware of the details. What the teacher will notice, however, are changes in your child's behaviour and emotional state.

Sometimes parents often think that they don't want to "trouble" the teacher with kids issues. You know what teachers tell me? They want to help their students feel safe and happy in school. Hence, do not hesitate to ask for help as soon as you suspect a problem.

6. Identify a trusted person

Every child needs a trusted person at school. Children spend the most of their days with their teachers and other kids. They need to know where they can go for help. They need a trusted person who would listen to them patiently without judging them. Help your child identify a trusted person at school who can help him if the bullying continues. Above all, provide a healthy environment for your child to talk to you by using active listening skills and showing your unconditional love for your child.

14 (iii) GOOD TOUCH BAD TOUCH

A lot has been written about danger strangers. This topic is the most important of all. Children should be made understood that they have to be very careful about the strangers. They cannot be friendly with them.

We need to educate and make our children understand properly about the "**good**" touch and the "**bad**" touch. Remember, out there is a big bad world, so it is our responsibility to make the children understand the importance of it.

Good Touch

When your own people hug you, it really feels good and one feels secure and loved. When mommy gives a big hug and a kiss, after you wake up. When Daddy reads a bedtime story and gives you a good-night hug and kiss. When grandparents come to visit and everyone gets hugs and kisses. This is good touch.

Bad Touch

A touch that makes you feel uncomfortable is definitely called a bad touch. Bad touch should not be kept secret. We as parents and teachers need to educate our children that if any incident of bad touch happens, they should immediately tell you. Make them understand that whoever gives them a bad touch is the one who is bad, not them. Explain them that their body belongs to themselves and no one should touch them if they don't want to be touched.

Educate them, what a bad touch is?

- If it hurts you, it is a bad touch.

- If someone touches you on your body where you don't want to be touched, it is a bad touch.
- If the person touches you under your clothing or tickles you under the clothing, then it is a bad touch.
- If a person touches you and that makes you feel uncomfortable, it is a bad touch.
- If that touch makes you feel scared and nervous, then, it is a bad touch.
- If a person forces you to touch him or her, then it is a bad touch.
- If a person asks you not to tell anyone, then definitely it is a bad touch.
- If a person threatens to hurt you if you tell them, it is a bad touch.

Teaching about Good Touch Bad Touch

Safety rules are very important and you should teach them the specific touching safety rules to your children.

1. **Children should know the correct names of all the different body parts, including their private parts.**

Children often find it hard to talk about ***sexual abuse*** because they don't know the words to use. Correct vocabulary or words (bodily) for body parts gives children the ease of using them. When teaching your young child the different body parts, consider using the correct words for private body parts along with words such as "tummy" and "ears." It will help them identify that it is fine to talk about private body parts.

Older children can be given more information because they are able to understand more. They can be explained in this way, that those parts that stay covered by a swimming costume are the private parts.

2. Teach children that "they own their body ,hence no one can touch it"

Teach them who can touch their body and how. Show them by doing it yourself, so that they can understand properly. If someone is trying to put them up and down, they should immediately say, "I don't want you to jump up and down on me. Please stop." You also make it clear politely that they need to stop tickling if the child says 'No'.

You can also let them know clearly that your child gives or receives hugs or kisses from relatives and friends only if they wish to. This gives the loud and clear message to children that it's okay to say no to touches from people in their family or other than family. You can very politely tell your relatives that you are teaching your children safety about touching, so they are not offended by your children's behaviour.

3. Make your child understand that there are three types of touches.

The three types of touches are:

Safe touches

The touches that keep our children safe and are full of care and love for them, and most importantly, make them feel loved and cared for.

All the touches which make you feel cared for, such as Safe hugging, pats on the back, and arms around the shoulders.

Sometimes safe touches might hurt like removing a bandage, putting ointment on a bruise or removing a splinter, but they are for taking care of your health and not to hurt you. So, they are a safe touch too.

Unsafe touches

These touches hurt children physically or emotionally like hitting, pushing, pinching, and kicking. Educate your children that these touches are unsafe and not acceptable. If such a situation arises with them, then it should be immediately brought to your (parents) notice.

Unwanted touches

These touches might be safe but a child doesn't want from that particular person or at that particular moment. It is the child's will to say "no" to an unwanted touch, even if it is from a familiar person. Your children need your guidance and help in learning to say "no" in a resilient yet polite voice. This will help children learn to set their personal restrictions. It is their right to say no if they don't want.

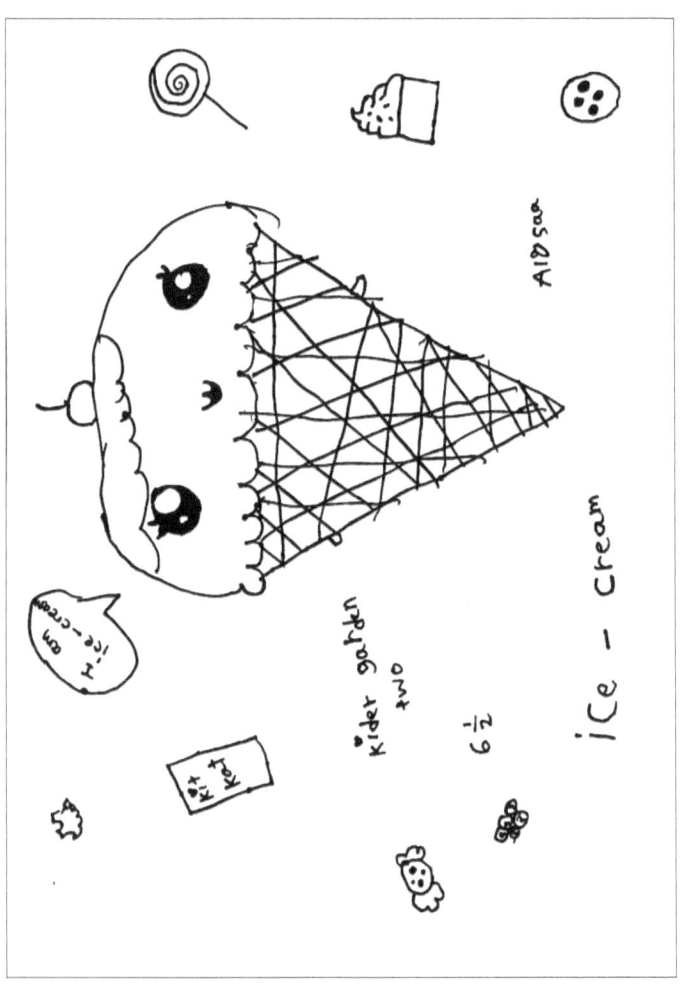

Message to the parents and adults such as relatives, neighbours and friends of the family:

It is sad, but some adults may exploit the trust you give them. If a person touches your child in an inappropriate manner, then it is the person who is doing something wrong, not your child. So, stand up and take action. Don't wait for the right time.

Epilogue

"Parents are the ultimate role models for children. Every word, movement and action have an effect.

No other person or outside force has a greater influence on a child than the parent."

Bob Keeshan

As it is rightly said, that we as parents need to play the active and ultimate role models in our child's life, development and education. We must get involved in their journey; it will assist them in making a smooth transition into better human beings. Parents should have more influence on children than any other means like friends or any form of media. Being a parent is like a privilege, cherish it. You do your bit and see the buds of love blooming into beautiful flowers.

www.ingramcontent.com/pod-product-compliance
Lightning Source LLC
LaVergne TN
LVHW041538070526
838199LV00046B/1716